MW01484093

TOUCH:
A ONE-ACT
PLAY

Briana Morgan

Copyright © 2016 Briana Morgan
All rights reserved.

ISBN: 069269420X
ISBN-13: 978-0692694206

All rights reserved. No part of this book may be used, reproduced or transmitted in any form or by any means, electronic or mechanical, including photocopying, recording by any information storage or retrieval system, without the written permission of the publisher, except where permitted by law, or in the case of brief quotations embodied in critical articles or reviews.

Visit the website for news and notices of upcoming releases at http://www.brianamaemorgan.com

For more information, contact BrianaMorgan@outlook.com

Published by Moran Publishing
11173 African Sunset Street
Henderson, NV 89052

TABLE OF CONTENTS

CHARACTERS

THE CURED—thirties/forties, the Seeker's mother

THE SEEKER—teenage girl, the Cured's daughter

THE ADDICT—woman of at least forty

THE DEALER—late twenties/early thirties

THE ENFORCER—mid-forties, the Cured's parole officer

PLACE

A city like any other, bustling and a little dirty.

TIME

The near future—or, perhaps, an alternate reality.

ACT ONE

Scene 1

Open on a woman, the SEEKER, sitting on a bed, looking embarrassed. Another woman, the CURED, her caregiver, reads from a diary. As she speaks, the SEEKER hangs her head in shame.

CURED.   *(Reading aloud.)* "I've never been hugged before. I don't know anyone who has. For as long as I can remember, the world has been full of people shying away from physical contact. There are no accidental touches without immediate apology, shame, and a little bit of fear. The law is meant to keep us safe. I know that as well as anyone does. Before touch was outlawed, virus and disease ran rampant. I know why the law exists. I know how it helps. Still, I wonder if the history of the human race is nothing but a list of 'thou shalt not's scribbled onto massive stone tablets. What was it like to touch someone on purpose? I wish I knew. I'd like to know. It isn't enough to imagine anymore. I need to go see for myself. (*She slams the diary shut and tosses it onto the bed.*) What do you have to say for yourself?

SEEKER. I didn't mean anything by it.

CURED. Then why did you write it?

SEEKER. I don't know.

CURED. You don't know?

SEEKER.   That was private. (*The CURED stares at her sternly without saying another word.*) It's my diary, all right? No one would have read it.

CURED. *I* read it.

SEEKER. You know what I mean.

CURED.   After everything I've been through... what were you thinking writing something like that? You know what could happen.

SEEKER.   Of course I do. I'm not an idiot.

CURED. You're acting like one.

SEEKER.   (*Sighing.*) I had a lot on my mind the other night. I couldn't sleep because my thoughts were driving me crazy. One of the girls at school said writing in a diary can help—

CURED. What girl at school?

SEEKER. Why does it matter?

CURED. Three of your classmates were arrested last week. How can you be so blind?

SEEKER. I'm not blind, Mother. I just choose not to see.

CURED. I don't see the difference.

SEEKER. The difference is choice. (*Beat.*) Those arrests were awful. They pulled them out of class and handcuffed them in the hallway. Sarah Cole *fainted*.

CURED. Those girls had it coming. They knew the risks.

SEEKER. No one deserves that.

CURED. They met in the woods to kiss. They were right behind the school. It was only a matter of time. I still can't believe they were stupid enough to—

SEEKER. They weren't stupid. They were *curious*. I think what they did was brave.

CURED. It wasn't brave. It was stupid. And you're being stupid now. (*She moves closer to the SEEKER.*) I don't want you to repeat my mistakes.

SEEKER. I'm sorry you think I'm stupid. I'm not stupid. I can't help noticing what's going on around me and I need some way to cope. The diary isn't hurting anyone. I want to keep it.

CURED. You can't keep it.

SEEKER. Why not?

CURED. We've been over this.

SEEKER. I keep it in the house. No one else has ever seen it.

CURED. Doesn't mean they never will. (*She sits down beside the SEEKER.*) It all starts with thinking. Then writing. The next thing you know, you're embracing a hug dealer and trying to explain to the police that you stumbled and he caught you—which, by the way, did not work for me.

SEEKER. Mother, that won't happen.

CURED. You don't know that.

SEEKER. I'm not you. (*She picks up the diary and holds it against her chest.*) I've been thinking and I want to meet my donor.

CURED. You can't.

SEEKER.   Doesn't City Hall keep records?

CURED. I don't even know who your donor is. It could be anyone. (*Beat.*) If you're not going to give me the diary, at least stop writing in it. Maybe tear out that last entry. I want you to be safe.

SEEKER. I'm sorry.

CURED. I know. (*The SEEKER gets up from the bed and crosses to the door. The CURED stands.*) Where are you going?

SEEKER.   Out. (*Lights fade as the SEEKER exits, leaving the CURED alone.*)

Scene 2

Lights up on an alley. A man is perched on top of a dumpster with a hood pulled over his face. He is the DEALER. The SEEKER sits on a bench on the other side of the stage, waiting for the bus and studying a map. She doesn't notice the DEALER. The ENFORCER enters, approaches the dumpster, and taps the side of it with his night stick.

DEALER. Can I help you, officer?

ENFORCER. Didn't I tell you to leave earlier?

DEALER. (*Ever the charmer*) Oh, I'm terribly sorry. You did indeed. Forgive me for not heeding your instructions. I would've moved on right away, if only it weren't for my leg...

ENFORCER. What's with your leg?

DEALER. War wound, sir. The pain flares up right before a big storm. (*Looking up at the sky.*) Look at that. Dark clouds. Just as I thought.

ENFORCER. Can you put weight on it? The leg, I mean.

DEALER. A little, but it's not good. (*Laying it on thick.*) People ask me if I would've gone to war knowing I'd come out like this. Of course I would have, I tell them. I wanted to serve my country. I would've taken a bullet through the heart while protecting this nation. I feel blessed to have only been shot in the leg. (*Sighing.*) You a veteran, officer?

ENFORCER. Oh, yes. It's nice to meet a fellow soldier.

DEALER. Likewise. (*He salutes. The ENFORCER salutes back.*)

ENFORCER. (*Smiling.*) Tell you what, pal—why don't we pretend I never told you to leave? There's no point irritating your injury. The streets are empty, so you won't bother anyone. The weather looks rough, though. Try to stay dry. (*He waves and exits.*)

DEALER. Thank you, officer. God bless you. (*After the ENFORCER is offstage, the DEALER hops down from the dumpster, pushing his hood back.*) Sucker. (*The*

DEALER goes around the side of the dumpster and pulls out a book. He begins reading. An ADDICT wanders onstage, groping along a wall. She is blind. She runs into the bench where the SEEKER is sitting.)

SEEKER. *(Startled.)* Oh!

ADDICT. Who's there?

SEEKER. *(Anxious.)* Just someone waiting for the bus.

ADDICT. I'd like to catch the bus as well. *(She feels along the top of the bench then down to the seat, finding it empty.)* Do you mind if I sit?

SEEKER. No. Go ahead. *(The ADDICT sits a little too close to the SEEKER. She scoots over. The ADDICT follows her lead until they're touching. The SEEKER leaps up, horrified.)* What are you doing?

ADDICT. What do you mean? (*Insistently.*) Why don't you sit back down? (*She stretches her hand toward the SEEKER, who shies away from the contact.*) What's wrong? Is there a policeman around?

SEEKER. That doesn't matter.

ADDICT. Do you see a policeman?

SEEKER. No.

ADDICT. All right then. What's the problem? (*She scoots. The SEEKER eyes her warily before sitting down. The ADDICT sits with her hands in her lap, humming. The SEEKER stares straight ahead, obviously unnerved by their interaction. The bus pulls up, engine humming. The SEEKER stands. The ADDICT scrambles to her feet, loses her balance, and grabs the SEEKER's arm to steady herself. The SEEKER supports her. The two of them freeze.*) Thank you.

SEEKER. Uh-huh. (*She steps away from the ADDICT and watches her get onto the bus. She decides not to get on. The ADDICT gets off the bus.*) What's going on?

ADDICT. I changed my mind. I think I'll walk. Want to walk with me?

SEEKER. (*Beat.*) Maybe for a little while.

ADDICT. Don't let me run into anything.

SEEKER. Okay. I'll try not to. (*The ADDICT takes her arm. She is startled but does not resist.*)

ADDICT. Thank you. See, I was thinking of heading towards East Street because there's that violin player on the corner... (*Her voice trails off as she hears the DEALER, who has begun singing to himself.*) Let's head this way.

SEEKER. Why? What's over there?

ADDICT. There's someone I think you should meet. (*The SEEKER leads the ADDICT to the other side of the stage, catching the DEALER's attention.*)

DEALER.   Ladies, welcome. What brings you two to my neck of the woods?

ADDICT. I know that voice.

DEALER. Don't say my name. (*He walks over to the ADDICT, taking her hand off the SEEKER's and putting it on his own. He covers her hand with his, and she leans into him.*) Let me guess. The usual?

ADDICT. Yes.

DEALER. (*Looking at the SEEKER*) And your pretty friend, what's she want from me?

SEEKER. (*Defensive.*) Nothing.

DEALER. (*Laughing.*) We'll see about that. Do you know who I am?

SEEKER. I can guess. You're a dealer.

DEALER. Smart girl. (*He winks and focuses on the ADDICT. She reaches into her pocket, takes out a few bills, and puts them in his hand.*) Perfect. (*He counts the money and puts it away. Satisfied, he takes the ADDICT by the shoulders and pulls her into a hug. The SEEKER gasps, but the pair ignores her. The hug lingers for several moments. The ADDICT reciprocates the embrace, swaying slightly. She touches the DEALER's cheek. He breaks the contact abruptly, taking several steps backward.*) You get what you pay for. No more. You know that.

ADDICT. Please, I need contact. Just touch my face.

DEALER. (*Firmly.*) Can you afford that?

ADDICT. Please. (*She lunges forward and he jumps back. She nearly topples over. The SEEKER rushes over to help her but the DEALER shakes his head.*)

DEALER. That's getting old. You're not that clumsy. (*She sinks to her knees.*) Get up. You're wasting my time. If you don't have any money, you don't get what you want.

ADDICT. One touch. Just one more.

DEALER. Don't make me call the cops.

ADDICT. You wouldn't do that. They'd arrest you.

DEALER. They love me. Granted, they don't know what I do, but the adore me nonetheless. (*To the ADDICT.*) Go on.

Get out of here. I'm sick of looking at you. (*The ADDICT buries her face in her hands, ashamed. She stands and exits without looking back. The SEEKER is conflicted. She neither advances toward nor retreats from the charismatic DEALER. He, on the other hand, comes closer to her. When he speaks again, his voice is warmer.*) What about you, sweetheart? You want something? First one's free.

SEEKER. I-I don't know. I don't think I should.

DEALER. That's the problem. You're thinking. You don't need to think. Just try it. (*He takes another step forward, holding a hand out to her. She reaches toward him but draws her hand back at the last second.*)

SEEKER. I'm sorry. I can't. I have to go home.

DEALER. Disappointing. (H*e takes a step forward, brushing his hand against her cheek. She leans into the contact.*) Rain check?

SEEKER. Sure thing. (*She lets the touch linger for a moment more. Then, she pulls away and exits. The DEALER looks after her. Lights fade.*)

Scene 3

Lights up on the SEEKER's bedroom. Through the window, we see lightning and rain. There is thunder. As for the SEEKER, she is sprawled out on her bed, writing in her diary. She is interrupted by a knock at the door and shoves the diary under her pillow. She forgets about the pen.

SEEKER. It's open. (*The CURED enters with a mug, which she sets down on the nearest flat surface.*) What's that?

CURED. Hot chocolate. It's still your favorite, right?

SEEKER. It's okay.

CURED. Since when don't you like it?

SEEKER. Since two years ago. (*She gets off the bed, picks up the mug, and gets back onto the bed.*) I drink coffee now.

CURED. I can take that away, then.

SEEKER. Forget it. It's fine.

CURED. (*Beat.*) You were writing in your diary.

SEEKER. No, I wasn't.

CURED. There's a pen on the bed. (*She walks over to the bed and takes the mug from her daughter.*) I'll go ahead and take this. If you go out again tonight, be careful. The rain is really coming down.

SEEKER. You're not going to forbid me from going anywhere?

CURED. It won't make any difference. (*She exits with the mug. The SEEKER resumes writing in her diary until her mother enters, carrying another mug.*) At least tell me you're being careful. Another entry like that last one could be your undoing.

SEEKER. I wish you'd stop worrying.

CURED. I'm your mother. I can't help it.

SEEKER. (*Taking the cup from the CURED.*) Can I ask you a question?

CURED. Of course.

SEEKER. (*Pause.*) Did you ever hold me when I was little?

CURED. (*Laughing.*) Does any mother *ever* hold her child?

SEEKER. Yeah, I guess that wouldn't make much sense. (*Pause.*) Oh, well. I was curious.

CURED. I haven't given you my answer. (*The SEEKER looks at her, intrigued.*) I did hold you once. Right after you were born. It wasn't for very long—the nurse took you from me right away—but I remember it. You were warm. You were... beautiful... (*Her voice trails off. She snaps out of her trance.*) That was the only time I ever touched you—on purpose, of course.

SEEKER.   Right. I got it. (*There is an uncomfortable beat. The SEEKER sips her drink, appeased. There is another flash of lightning and crash of thunder. The SEEKER straightens, alert.*) "Rain check," he said.

CURED. Who said?

SEEKER.   It's pouring. (*She sets the mug aside, gets down from the bed, and exits. The CURED goes over to the pillow and finds the diary. She toys with the idea of reading it, changes her mind, slips it back under the pillow, and exits. Lights fade.*)

Scene 4

Lights up on the alley. The DEALER is perched on the dumpster again, unaffected by the rain. He is whistling an upbeat tune in spite of the weather. The SEEKER enters, toting an umbrella. She is anxious. He notices her right away and jumps down from the dumpster.

DEALER. What have we here? Back so soon?

SEEKER. Just following up on that rain check. Do you remember me?

DEALER. Of course. So... What can I do for you?

SEEKER. I'm not sure. I mean, I have an idea, but I'm open to suggestions.

DEALER. If you'd rather not do this out in the streets—

SEEKER. Do I have a choice?

DEALER. Always. (*He takes a step toward the SEEKER. She steps closer to him and holds her umbrella over both of them.*) We can go to my place. (*He takes the umbrella from her and puts his arm around her. She flinches.*) It's all right. Relax.

SEEKER. (*She lets him put his arm around her.*) I haven't paid you yet.

DEALER. I told you, first one's free. (*They start to exit. The CURED enters. The DEALER drops his arm and breaks away from the SEEKER.*)

CURED. What are you doing?

DEALER. The young lady was lost. I was giving her directions.

SEEKER. (*To the DEALER.*) Forget it. She's my mother. (*To the CURED.*) How did you find me?

CURED. I read your diary. I didn't want to, but I was worried. I paced back and forth in the living room for fifteen minutes trying to resist the temptation to snoop. But then I thought about those girls from your school who got arrested. I remembered what I was like at your age. I thought about my affair, the arrest, the trial, prison, rehab—I *had* to come after you. I needed to rescue you. So I read your diary. (*She looks at the DEALER.*) Have you done anything?

DEALER. Not yet.

CURED. What do you mean, not yet?

DEALER. We were interrupted.

CURED. You're in the process?

DEALER. Yes.

CURED. Has she paid you yet?

DEALER. No.

CURED. Thank God.

DEALER. She doesn't have to. Pay, I mean. She can thank God if she wants to. That's her decision. (*He winks at the SEEKER. The CURED bristles.*)

CURED. Forget whatever arrangement you have. There isn't going to be any transaction.

SEEKER. You don't have any say in this.

CURED. You're kidding me, right? I'm your *mother*. I gave birth to you. You're a minor living under my roof, and if you don't want to face some serious consequences—

SEEKER. The most you can do is ground me.

CURED. No, the *least* I can do is ground you. The most I can do is turn you over to the police. (*The tension between mother and daughter is palpable. It's palpable and thick. It is clear that the CURED has gone too far, said the unthinkable. The relationship between the two of them will never be the same. The CURED senses this and, terrified, tries to backpedal.*) Oh, honey, no. No no no. I didn't mean that. I would *never.* (*The SEEKER, determined, wanders over to the DEALER, slips her arm through his, and rests her head on his shoulder.*)

SEEKER. Go home, Mother.

CURED. (*Taken aback.*) You know I only want what's best for you.

SEEKER.   Maybe *this* is best for me. Maybe I need to see what it's like for myself. Maybe it's not enough to hear all the reasons why I *shouldn't* without learning if I *should.* (*Pause.*) Maybe you should head back before somebody sees you. Don't want to violate parole. (*The CURED stares at her daughter, almost looking right through her. She reacts as though she had been slapped, staggering backward, pausing, and trying to collect herself. Then, having come to terms with what she is about to do, she pivots on her heel and exits. The DEALER puts his arms around the SEEKER and she leans in. He kisses her. Lights fade as they kiss and thunder rumbles overhead.)*

Scene 5

Lights up on a dilapidated apartment. There are a few pieces of cheap furniture and a dirty mattress on the floor. A tower of books leans against the wall, on the verge of toppling over. Several more books are scattered throughout the apartment. There are the only things that look new, clean, and cared-for. A single window with ratty curtains looks out over the city. The room is illuminated by lightning and street lights coming in through the window. The DEALER unlocks the door and holds it open for the SEEKER. Once she is inside, he shuts the door and locks it. The SEEKER surveys her new surroundings.

SEEKER. *(Sarcastically.)* You sure know how to impress a girl.

DEALER. Who said it was impressive? Convenient, I said, and safe. Never impressive.

SEEKER. It's dry. That's what counts. Do you bring many customers here?

DEALER. You're the first.

SEEKER. You're kidding.

DEALER. Are you surprised?

SEEKER. Am I special?

DEALER. In general or to me?

SEEKER. You know what I'm asking.

DEALER. I told you, you're the first one I've brought back to my place. (*He goes over to the mattress and pushes a pile of books to the floor.*) Sorry for the mess. I'm a bibliophile.

SEEKER. You're a what?

DEALER. A bibliophile. Book lover. It's my secret shame, my cross to bear. What about you? Any secrets to confess?

SEEKER. Nothing comes to mind.

DEALER. Come on. There must be something.

SEEKER. I write in a diary.

DEALER. That the best you've got?

SEEKER. I write a lot about touch. The idea of contact. I like to make up scenarios in which someone accidentally brushes against me and lingers a little too long to be appropriate. (*Pause.*) I dream about it, too, sometimes. I write those down as well. My mother found my diary the other day and she freaked out. She doesn't want me getting caught up in the idea of—well, you know. You saw how she acted.

DEALER. You knew she was reading your diary and you still wrote about me. Why?

SEEKER. I had to tell someone about you.

DEALER. I see. (*He gestures to the mattress.*) Have a seat, if you want. It's not as dirty as it looks. It's just somebody's cast-off. I got it at the—okay, I guess it doesn't matter. (*Hesitantly, she sits down. He*

sits down beside her. They are not touching.)
How are you feeling?

SEEKER. Nervous more than anything.

DEALER. You should be.

SEEKER. Gee, thanks.

DEALER. I mean it. (*He touches her arm. She doesn't flinch this time.*) I want you to know what you're getting yourself into. There are significant risks involved in our little arrangement. I hate to even say this, but should we get caught... you and I could both be facing serious jail time.

SEEKER. Ten years is ten years. It'll pass all the same.

DEALER. Ten years for you would be fifteen for me—that is, if I'm lucky.

SEEKER. And what if you're not?

DEALER. Maybe twenty or thirty. Life in prison, even. (*Beat.*) Needless to say, there's a great deal at stake.

SEEKER. Do you think it's worth it?

DEALER. I don't know. Do you?

SEEKER. (*She covers his hand with hers, smiling.*) Where do we go from here?

DEALER. Wherever you like. You said you had some ideas?

SEEKER. Only a few.

DEALER. I can work with a few. After that, we can improvise. (*He touches her face, strokes her hair, and slides his hands down her arms. She takes her hands in his and interlaces their fingers. She grins.*)

SEEKER. I've been dying to try this. Holding hands. I saw it in a movie once.

DEALER. What movie? I thought they edited all of them.

SEEKER. It was a long time ago, when I was a toddler. My mother found a video disc in her closet. She put it into the player and skipped to the part where the couple was holding hands, standing on a hill, looking out over a city. She kept replaying that scene, over and over, and then she started crying. I didn't know why. Her parole officer found the disc a little later but decided, for some reason, not to report her. That's all I remember.

DEALER. Your mom was an addict?

SEEKER. One of the first. She used to say that like it was something to be proud of. After some girls at my school got arrested, though… She told me the most awful stories of things she'd seen in prison, people at rehab, stuff like that. She didn't want me to end up like her. She didn't want me seeking some attention from a dealer.

DEALER. Hence the tension in the alley.

SEEKER. Right. That was awful. (*She drops her hands from his and pulls him into a hug. He embraces her tightly, continuing to hold her when she doesn't pull away.*)

DEALER. Does this feel good to you?

SEEKER. It does.

DEALER. It does to me, too. Was there anything else that you wanted to try?

SEEKER. There was one thing.

DEALER.   What? (*She pulls away and smiles shyly. He returns the smile.*) I bet I could guess.

SEEKER. You could definitely guess. (*He leans in and kisses her full on the mouth. She melts into the contact. They continue kissing and lie down on the mattress.*)

DEALER. Am I getting warm?

SEEKER. Very.

DEALER. Are you sure you want to do this?

SEEKER.   No, but I *do* want to. I'm scared and excited. (*Pause.*) I trust you.

DEALER. I'm glad. (*He leans over her and they kiss again. Lights fade.*)

Scene 6

Lights up on the DEALER's apartment, an hour or so later. The SEEKER is sitting up on the mattress, clutching a blanket to her chest. The DEALER, in his boxers, rummages through a stack of books.

SEEKER. Are you sure it's in that pile?

DEALER. It may look like chaos, but it's organized chaos. I know where everything is. It's got to be here.

SEEKER. What about the books you pushed off the mattress?

DEALER. I haven't had it that recently. (*He continues rummaging through the pile of books. The SEEKER leans over and picks a book up off the floor.*)

SEEKER. I think I found it.

DEALER. Where?

SEEKER. On the floor like I told you. (*She reads the title.*) "The Holy Bible." Wait. This can't be real. I thought these were all destroyed?

DEALER. I bought a copy from an art dealer several years ago. Do you know why it was destroyed? (*He goes over to the mattress and sits back down beside her. She pulls the blanket over both of them.)*

SEEKER.   Objectionable   content.   Is there touching?

DEALER. Oh, yes. *(He takes the Bible from her, flips to a passage, and begins to read aloud.)* "And there was a woman who had had a discharge of blood for twelve years, and though she had spent all her living on physicians, she could not be healed by anyone. She came up behind Jesus and touched the hem of his garment, and immediately her discharge of blood ceased. And Jesus said, 'Who was it that touched me?' When all denied it, Peter said, 'Master, the crowds surround you and are pressing in on you.' But Jesus said, 'Someone touched me, for I perceive that power has gone out from me.' And when the woman saw that she was not hidden, she came trembling, and falling down before him declared in the presence of all the people why she had touched him, and how she had been immediately healed. And he said to her, 'Daughter, your faith has made you well; go in peace.'"

SEEKER. She wasn't supposed to touch him.

DEALER. No, but he still healed her.

SEEKER. All she had to do was touch him.

DEALER. Contact, my dear, is a powerful thing. Don't you agree?

SEEKER. I do. (*She leans in and kisses him. The contact is gentle, not rushed. When they pull apart, the DEALER strokes the SEEKER's hair.*) Why are you looking at me like that?

SEEKER. Like I'm beautiful.

DEALER. Because you are.

SEEKER. I bet you say that to all of your customers.

DEALER. Some of them, but never here. You're different. I've never felt for anyone the way I feel for you. (*The SEEKER gets up from the mattress, dresses, and begins to gather her belongings.*) Hey, what's the rush? Where are you going?

SEEKER. Home. My mother's going to freak out if I stay with you another minute. We don't want her calling the police.

DEALER. Can't you stay a little longer?

SEEKER. No way. I'm sorry.

DEALER. I have more books to read to you.

SEEKER. I wish I could stay. I have to get home. (*She stoops to kiss him.*)

DEALER. Will I see you again?

SEEKER.   Do you usually set up appointments for this?

DEALER. Sweetheart, there's nothing *usual* where you and I are concerned. Tell me straight—are you willing to do this again?

SEEKER. This?

DEALER. Us.

SEEKER. Oh, yes. Most definitely yes.

DEALER.   Then I am *most definitely* looking forward to that. Until then, beautiful.

SEEKER. (*She starts toward the door, pauses in the doorway, and turns back to him.*) I know you said this one was on the house, but next time, how do I...?

DEALER. (*Shaking his head.*) There won't be a need.

SEEKER. I'm your customer. I want to pay you.

DEALER. Given what you do to me, I should be paying *you*. (*He winks.*) If you're so insistent on paying me... Well, you could always bring me a book.

SEEKER. I wouldn't be able to get you one that hasn't been edited.

DEALER. Doesn't matter that much. I have several of those. Most of the time I can guess what they've taken out, anyway, so it's almost like they haven't taken out anything at all. They can take away what turns us on, but they can't take away arousal. It's human nature, sweetheart. (*A siren goes off nearby. The DEALER and SEEKER freeze, exchanging nervous glances.*) Must be getting close to curfew. They're out looking for stragglers.

SEEKER. Curfew. I forgot. It's going to take me half an hour to get home if the buses have stopped running. What am I supposed to do?

DEALER. Have you ever violated curfew before?

SEEKER. Before you, I never so much as jaywalked.

DEALER. Okay, then, you're set. Just say you got lost or held up or something. Pretty girl like you... They'll give you a warning. "Just don't let it happen again" and the like.

SEEKER. You sure about that?

DEALER. I break curfew all the time. I've learned all the tips and tricks to avoid getting charged. Unfortunately, you can only ever get one warning, but you don't need to be worried about that. There are other ways around the law. I hope you'll never need them.

SEEKER. (*Looking him over.*) I already do.

DEALER. Yeah, I guess you're right. (*He walks over to her and kisses her again. The embrace lingers, no longer just business. Then, before she can second-guess herself, the SEEKER slips out of his arms and out the door. The DEALER locks it behind her, smiling. Another siren goes off as the SEEKER steps into the alley. The SEEKER sneaks around a corner, glancing over her shoulder to make sure she isn't being followed. The ENFORCER enters while her back is turned, making his rounds, and notices the SEEKER.*)

ENFORCER. Hold it right there, miss. What are you doing out here?

SEEKER. Please, sir. I got lost. I didn't mean to be out here so late. I know it's after curfew.

ENFORCER. Got lost, you say?

SEEKER. Yes, sir.

ENFORCER. How did you get lost?

SEEKER. *(Hesitantly.)* Well, sir, I was walking along East Street when it started to rain. The sky opened up. You remember that, don't you? *(He nods.)* Right. So. When it started pouring, I went running for cover. And I don't know how it happened but... Somehow I got all turned around. *(Pause.)* Now I don't know where I am. I want to go home.

ENFORCER.   I'll take you home. Where do you live?

SEEKER.   Corner of Red and Stanton. Big brownstone complex. It's on the—

ENFORCER.   Yeah, I know it. I'm the parole officer for a woman who lives there. (*He studies her for a moment.*) Have we met before?

SEEKER.   Not that I can remember.

ENFORCER.   You sure about that? (*There is a long pause.*)

SEEKER.   I never forget a face. Lead the way, officer. (*They start offstage. Lights fade.*)

Scene 7

Lights up on the living room of the SEEKER's apartment. The SEEKER and the ENFORCER enter through the front door. The CURED is nowhere to be seen.

SEEKER. You don't have to stay. I'm fine now. I appreciate you walking me home, but I'm fine.

ENFORCER. I'd still like to have a word with your guardian, if you don't mind. Lost or not, you were still out after curfew. (*Pause.*) Say, this apartment looks familiar... What did you say your mother did for a living?

SEEKER. She's a book editor.

ENFORCER. Tough job, I hear. Works long hours, doesn't she? The women in my charge, she—

SEEKER. If it's all the same to you, I'd rather not make small talk. I'm very tired and I'd like to go to bed as soon as possible. (*She sits down on the couch. The ENFORCER follows her, much to her chagrin.*) Don't you have rounds to make or something like that? I'd hate to keep you from your work.

ENFORCER.   I'm on curfew enforcement duty tonight. I'm doing work right now.

SEEKER. Fantastic.

CURED. (*Offstage.*) What are you doing back so late? It's way past curfew.

ENFORCER. That your mother?

SEEKER. Yeah. She's going to lecture me for sure. You better get out while you still have a chance.

ENFORCER. Hold on. Maybe she'll feel better after I reassure her you were lost. Besides, I think that voice—

SEEKER. No need. She won't listen. She never listens when she's angry.

CURED. (*Still offstage.*) You need to change into some dry clothes so you don't catch a cold.

ENFORCER. She doesn't sound angry.

SEEKER. You really should go. (*The CURED walks into the room. She sees the ENFORCER and freezes in her tracks.*)

ENFORCER. (*Standing.*) You're her mother?

CURED. Of course I am.

SEEKER. What's going on?

CURED. This is… my parole officer.

ENFORCER. (*To the SEEKER.*) I knew this place looked familiar. (*To the CURED.*) Your daughter was out past her curfew. Normally, I'd let her off with just a warning, but since your family has a history of physical contact… I'm afraid I'll have to detain her for a round of questioning. Standard protocol for this kind of sensitive situation.

CURED. You're going to arrest her?

SEEKER. I haven't done anything.

ENFORCER. Your mother's done enough for both of you. (*Taking out a pair of handcuffs.*) Hands behind your back. Don't make this more difficult than it has to be. (*The SEEKER does as she's told. Before the ENFORCER can put the handcuffs on her, the CURED grabs a vase, rushes forward, and smacks the ENFORCER's head. He drops.*)

SEEKER. You hit him.

CURED. Get out. Go.

SEEKER. You'll go to prison.

CURED. I know I will. (*There is a long pause.*) Please. Get out of here. I love you. (*The SEEKER touches her mother's arm and moves to embrace her, but she shakes her head.*) Go now.

SEEKER.   I love you, Mother. Thank you. (*The SEEKER exits. The CURED goes over to the couch, sits down, and puts the vase in her hands. Lights fade.*)

Scene 8

Lights up on the DEALER's apartment. He is sleeping on the mattress, shirtless. The SEEKER pounds on the door. The DEALER groans but does not stir. There is more knocking. He leaps up, looks through the peephole, and opens the door. The SEEKER rushes past him without so much as a greeting.

SEEKER. *(Frantic.)* I tried to stay out of sight on the way back but I ran into an enforcer and he didn't suspect anything between us but I lied and told him I was lost and he brought me back home and he's my mother's parole officer and he was going to arrest me and she hit him with a vase and I panicked and I didn't know where else to go I just— (*He stops her words with a kiss. She is initially stunned by the contact but soon relaxes into it.*) I'm sorry. I'm so sorry.

DEALER. Don't be sorry. It's okay. It's all going to be fine. (*He holds her close, stroking her hair.*) Take a deep breath. Try telling me again.

SEEKER. I was headed back when I ran into an enforcer. I tried to get away from him using an excuse, saying I got lost, and he just offered to help me find my way home. When we got to my apartment, he recognized my mother. He's her parole officer. He threatened to take me down to the police station for some questioning and my mom knocked

him out with a vase. I ran straight here. I
don't know what to do.

DEALER. Hey, that's all right. I meant
it when I said you're going to be fine.
You trust me, don't you?

SEEKER. With my life.

DEALER. That's all I needed to hear.
(*Before the SEEKER can say another word, the
DEALER begins throwing stuff in a duffel bag
resting on the mattress. The Bible goes in first,
followed by some other books, and then finally
some clothing. He closes the bag and pulls it onto
his shoulder.*)

SEEKER. I'm going with you.

DEALER. It's too dangerous.

SEEKER. It's more dangerous here. I'm
going.

DEALER. You're running away with me? Sweetheart, you just met me.

SEEKER. You've changed my life. You've changed everything. Nothing can ever be the same for me, and I don't want it to be. I don't want to ever live without touch again. I owe you more than I can say.

DEALER. All I did was touch you.

SEEKER. Exactly my point. (*They look at each other for a long time. The DEALER stops putting things in his bag. He sets it down on the couch and crosses over to where the SEEKER is standing. She doesn't move. He wraps his arms around her and hugs her. She hugs him back.*) Does this mean I can go with you?

DEALER. It's out of my hands. The minute I saw you, I was in trouble. I think I'd let you follow me to the ends of the earth and beyond if you wanted.

SEEKER. That settles it.

DEALER. Once again, I want to make sure you know what you're getting into.

SEEKER. I know.

DEALER. You'll have to give up whatever else is here for you—school, work, your family... You won't be able to come back.

SEEKER. I know.

DEALER. You probably won't be able to talk to anyone here once we get where we're going. Can't give ourselves away.

SEEKER. I get it.

DEALER. Fair enough. You've said your goodbyes?

SEEKER. More or less. I... I wanted to give my mother something before we left, if there's any time.

DEALER. There might be. What is it?

SEEKER. It's nothing. I wanted to give her a hug. (*The apartment is quiet for a long time. The DEALER smiles.*)

DEALER. I think we can do that. Let me finish packing up and then we'll head to your place. (*The SEEKER smiles him as she watches him return to packing his bag. She goes over to him and interrupts him by kissing him on the mouth. When she pulls away, he grins. Lights fade.*)

Scene 9

Lights up on the SEEKER's apartment. The DEALER and the SEEKER are sitting on the couch, staring straight ahead. They are holding hands. There is no one else in the apartment. The place has been ransacked.

SEEKER. I should've known we'd be too late.

DEALER. Maybe she wasn't taken in. Maybe she left of her own volition. She had no idea you were coming back here.

SEEKER. No, she was arrested. If she'd gone somewhere the enforcer's body would still be here. He was unconscious when I left. She couldn't have dragged him off; he was too heavy. Maybe he called for backup.

DEALER. Or something. You know, I didn't get to say goodbye to my mother, either.

SEEKER. You ran away from home?

DEALER. They took home away. A bunch of enforcers had bugged our house and heard me talking to my mother about hug dealing. I was out with some friends, came back late... everything was ashes. They burned the whole place down.

SEEKER. And your mother?

DEALER. I don't know. I'll never know what happened. She could still be alive. Maybe they took her to prison or she got away somehow. Maybe she served time and now she's living somewhere far away where people still shake hands.

SEEKER. No one tracked you down?

DEALER. I don't even think they tried to. Like I said, they'd put microphones in our house. They knew what I wanted to do. When I went out that night, we were at a bar in the middle of town. They could've gotten me then if they'd wanted to.

SEEKER. But they got your house instead.

DEALER. They wanted to scare me. I wish it had worked. (*He kisses her hand.*) I'm worried about you. If something happens to us, they're going to take you. They'll do anything they can to get under my skin. Do you understand?

SEEKER. They'll torture me, maybe kill me, just to hurt you?

DEALER. That's right.

SEEKER. But why wouldn't they just cart you off to prison or something?

DEALER. Human nature is so much darker than anything you can imagine. Before, when we had touch, people were able to keep some of their madness contained, but now... Prison's not enough of a punishment for me. They know it hurts me more for them to hurt people I care about.

SEEKER. Do you think that's why they wanted to take me in? To hurt my mother?

DEALER. Absolutely.

SEEKER. When they couldn't get me, they got her anyway. It made no difference to them in the end. I wish I could've said goodbye at least. I wish I could've hugged her.

DEALER. I'm so sorry.

SEEKER. I'm sorry, too. (*Pause.*) My whole childhood I felt so completely alone. So cold. I ached. I wanted someone to acknowledge me, and not just with their words. I felt invisible. I didn't exist. That's why I wanted to hug my mother. To make her feel seen. (*Pause.*) Is touch so powerful?

DEALER. You know. (*He kisses her. The SEEKER gets up from the couch to grab the vase from the table by the door. She holds the vase against her chest and looks at the DEALER.*)

SEEKER. Let's get out of here. (*The DEALER gets up from the couch and walks over to the SEEKER. He puts his arm around her and they exit together. Blackout.*)

End of Play

ABOUT THE AUTHOR

Briana Morgan is a YA and NA writer, editor, and blogger who loves dark, suspenseful reads, angst-ridden relationships, and complicated characters. Her interest in Jay Gatsby scares her friends and family. You can find her in way too many places online, eating too much popcorn, reading in the corner, or crying about long-dead literary heroes.

Made in the USA
Columbia, SC
19 September 2020

21199649R00043